Anne Fine, aged twelve, once asked her teacher 'Could I be a writer?'

'Oh, yes,' the teacher replied. '<u>You</u> could.'

How right she was! Anne went on to become a very successful writer indeed.

D1485921

Anne outside her house in County Durham.

Anne Fine is the author of more than forty books for children, as well as six books for adults. She's won a stack of prizes. One book, "Madame Doubtfire", was made into a blockbuster Hollywood film. Others have been made into television programmes. And from 2001-2003, Anne was Children's Laureate (perhaps the biggest prize of all).

▼ A video…

ROBIN WILLIAMS   SALLY FIELD

MRS. DOUBTFIRE

PG

GREAT SAVINGS

MRS. DOUBTFIRE

▲…and a T-shirt. Both are spin-offs from a best-selling book.

Maybe surprisingly, Anne's family wasn't especially book-ish. Her father was busy being an electrical engineer. Her mother was busy being a Mum. Anne was the second of five girls – the last three were triplets.

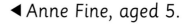
◄ Anne Fine, aged 5.

▼ The five sisters – Elizabeth, Anne, Bridget, Sally and Nina.

Anne spent the early years of her childhood on a new housing estate in Hampshire. When she was seven, her family moved to a bigger house. 'It was flint-fronted, ugly and dark and overlooked a graveyard – perfect for a haunting.'

▼ The house Anne moved to at the age of seven.

▲ The ghost story based on this house that Anne wrote as a grown-up.

Anne's next home with its lovely garden.

Later on, Anne's family moved again. This house had a beautiful garden. 'It was large and walled. I spent whole days on that wall. It was a favourite place for reading.'

Already, Anne was a keen reader. 'I read everywhere at that age,' she says. 'On the wall. On the grass. In the bath. On buses. Standing in line... it's not tests or exercises that turn you into a writer. It's reading, reading...and more reading!'

Luckily, she knew a superb storyteller as well. It was her own Granny Bertha. 'She had no regard for truth at all, so far as I could tell. All through her life she told the most frightful whoppers...and every story she told was wonderful.' Listening to her granny taught Anne a lot. It was her love of reading and Granny Bertha that made her become a writer.

▶ Granny Bertha with the five girls. Anne is the one in front.

◀ Anne in her school nativity play – already a star!

Apart from maths and needlework, Anne did well at school. Next came Warwick University, where she studied history and politics. Soon afterwards, she married the philosopher Kit Fine. Eventually, his job took them to Edinburgh. At first, Anne didn't like being so far from friends and family. To cheer herself up, she wrote a book.

A view of Edinburgh.

Anne's first book was called "The Summer House Loon". She kept it tucked away under her bed for three years, until she entered it in a competition for new writers. It came third and was published. By then, Anne and Kit had moved first to America and then Canada. They also had two daughters called Ione and Cordelia. Later, Anne and Kit split up.

Anne's first partner, Kit, with their daughters Cordelia (aged 8) and Ione (aged 12).

▼ Just two of Anne's mountain of medals.

▲ Anne is always happy to write about dogs. Her present dog is called Henry.

Was it possible to carry on writing while bringing up two daughters on her own? Somehow, back in Edinburgh, Anne managed it. Books like "Goggle Eyes", "Flour Babies" and "The Tulip Touch" began to win prizes. So did her books for younger readers, like "Bill's New Frock" and "How To Write Really Badly". Anne even wrote some picture books, "Poor Monty" for instance, and "Ruggles".

These days, there are Anne Fine stories for every age. But whether a story is "Up On Cloud Nine" (best for teenagers) or "Notso-Hotso" (best for young readers), it'll be funny and make you think. In "Goggle Eyes", one of the characters says "...life is a long and doggy business. And stories and books help. Some help you with the living itself. Some help you just take a break. The best do both at the same time."

Anne's books are the best kind.

Two books for Anne's older readers – to help with living while making them laugh.

14

Nowadays Anne lives in the north of England with her partner, Dick Warren. Their house is big and rambling. It needs to be, too. Like Anne, Dick earns his living by doing what he likes best. He grows rare flowers called orchids. He sends them all over the world to other orchid lovers.

▲ Dick in his orchid workshop.

◀ Growing orchids can be as tricky as writing a book.

15

Anne doesn't need quite as much space. Even so, her bright, sunny study gives her lots of room to spread out. 'I work in absolute silence,' she says, 'apart from my own mutterings.'

Mostly, she writes her stories out by hand. Later, she transfers them on to a computer.

Anne in the new workroom she had built on to her house.

Anne's dog Henry in the snow.

Here's how Anne spends her working day:

7.00am: Wake up. Read the papers in bed with my tea.

8.00 – 9.00am: Walk the dog. Have breakfast.

9.00 – 10.00am: Clear urgent letters and faxes.

10.00am – 4.00pm: Writing…eating lunch at my desk (this often makes my pages very colourful!)

4.00pm: Read in the bath. Walk the dog again.

5.00pm-ish: Back to the letters and faxes.

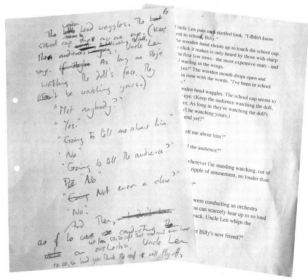

The first draft of an Anne Fine story…and the typed-up version which followed.

17

Anne's in-tray is always crammed with these letters and faxes. Once, they were piled so high they collapsed on her! Now she has two in-trays.

Lately though, they've been piled higher than ever. In 2001, Anne was made Children's Laureate. This is a bit like being declared president of the country's children's books.

Anne meeting some of her fans at a school.

As Laureate, Anne has launched two projects very dear to her. The first was a reminder of how enjoyable the best poetry can be, especially when learned by heart. The second, promoted on World Book Day in 2002, was to make children proud of owning books. 'Why not use the internet to download special bookplates free of charge?' Anne suggested.

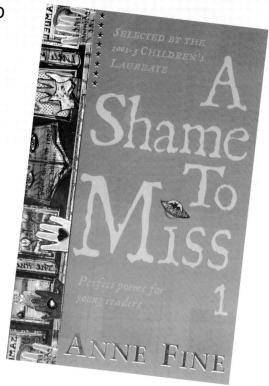

▲A book of poems Anne would love children not to miss.

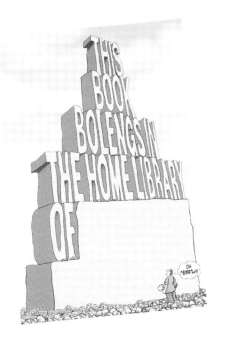

◄A bookplate you can download for yourself from www.myhomelibrary.org

Already, thousands of children all over the world have taken up her offer. Maybe one day some of them will go on to ask 'Could I be a writer?'

Of course, most of them won't have a Granny Bertha to show them how. But they can all try 'reading, reading...and more reading.' It worked brilliantly for Anne Fine.

Anne Fine, Children's Laureate.

Important dates

1947	Anne Fine is born
1950	Anne starts infant school a year early – her mother is busy with the triplets!
1953-54	Anne is too young for the junior school. She spends the year 'reading, reading and more reading'
1958	Anne starts secondary school
1965-68	Goes to Warwick University
1968	Anne marries Kit Fine
1969-80	Anne moves to Scotland, America and Canada
1971	Ione is born
1975	Cordelia is born
1978	Anne's first book is published ("The Summer House Loon")
1989	Anne wins her first Carnegie Medal (for "Google Eyes")
1992	Anne wins another Carnegie Medal (for "Flour Babies")
2001-03	Anne is appointed Children's Laureate

Keywords

apprentice someone learning a craft or a skill

blockbuster a film that is successful worldwide

bookplate a label to say who owns a book

Carnegie Medal Britain's top prize for a children's book

Children's Laureate Britain's top children's author (appointed for a two-year period)

philosopher someone who studies knowledge and wisdom

spin-off things that follow from a popular book such as a video, or toy, or T-shirt

Index